Assertiveness Skills

Assertiveness Skills

NELDA SHELTON

SHARON BURTON

The Business Skills Express Series

BUSINESS ONE IRWIN/MIRROR PRESS
Burr Ridge, Illinois
New York, New York
Boston, Massachusetts

© RICHARD D. IRWIN, INC., 1994

This publication is designed to provide accurate and authoritative information in regard to the subject matter covered. It is sold with the understanding that neither the author nor the publisher is engaged in rendering legal, accounting, or other professional service. If legal advice or other expert assistance is required, the services of a competent professional person should be sought.

From a Declaration of Principles jointly adopted by a Committee of the American Bar Association and a Committee of Publishers.

Mirror Press:	David R. Helmstadter
	Carla F. Tishler
Editor-in-Chief:	Jeffrey A. Krames
Project editor:	Mary Vandercar
Production manager:	Bob Lange
Designer:	Jeanne M. Rivera
Art coordinator:	Heather Burbridge
Compositor:	Alexander Graphics
Typeface:	12/14 Criterion
Printer:	Malloy Lithographing, Inc.

Library of Congress Cataloging-in-Publication Data

Shelton, Nelda.
    Assertiveness skills / Nelda Shelton, Sharon Burton.
      p.   cm. — (Business skills express)
    ISBN 1-55623-857-6
    1. Assertiveness (Psychology) 2. Assertiveness training.
  3. Psychology, Industrial. 4. Interpersonal relations. I. Burton,
Sharon. II. Title. III. Series.
    BF575.A85S56 1994
    158'.2—dc20   93–18310

Printed in the United States of America
1 2 3 4 5 6 7 8 9 ML 0 9 8 7 6 5 4 3

PREFACE

Assertiveness Skills teaches assertiveness concepts through practical exercises that involve the reader in hands-on activities. You will gain an understanding that assertive behavior is a skill that can be learned and maintained. When you develop positive assertiveness, you will gain self-knowledge, be able to express yourself clearly, and get where you want to be in your career.

This book will give you the confidence to make yourself heard. You'll learn positive, empowering techniques to ensure that your contributions to meetings, conferences, and day-to-day office interaction are sought after and noticed. Above all, you'll learn to speak up for yourself with grace and confidence.

Nelda Shelton
Sharon Burton

ABOUT THE AUTHORS

Nelda Shelton, Associate Professor at Tarrant County Junior College in Texas, is an expert in office systems technology. As a consultant, Ms. Shelton conducts workshops and seminars on communication and office skills, as well as career development, customer service, listening and memory development, and business and technical writing. Ms. Shelton has consulted for the U.S. Office of Personnel Management and the Communications and Office Skills Institute.

Sharon Burton is a Professor of Office Technology at Brookhaven College in Texas. Her experience includes consulting and training for the Texas Coordinating Board, the U.S. Information Agency, and the U.S. Office of Personnel Management. Ms. Burton specializes in assertiveness training, curriculum development and teaching strategies, communication skills, and computer technology.

Nelda Shelton and Sharon Burton have co-authored more than 15 books on office technology and computer applications.

ABOUT BUSINESS ONE IRWIN

Business One Irwin is the nation's premier publisher of business books. As a Times Mirror company, we work closely with Times Mirror training organizations, including Zenger-Miller, Inc., Learning International, Inc., and Kaset International, to serve the training needs of business and industry.

About the Business Skills Express Series

This expanding series of authoritative, concise, and fast-paced books delivers high-quality training on key business topics at a remarkably affordable cost. The series will help managers, supervisors, and front-line personnel in organizations of all sizes and types hone their business skills while enhancing job performance and career satisfaction.

Business Skills Express books are ideal for employee seminars, independent self-study, on-the-job training, and classroom-based instruction. Express books are also convenient-to-use references at work.

CONTENTS

Self-Assessment

Respond to the following statements by assessing your current thoughts and feelings. This will alert you to areas to work on.

	Almost Always	Sometimes	Almost Never
1. I can express my feelings openly to others.	_____	_____	_____
2. When a person treats me unfairly, I call attention to it.	_____	_____	_____
3. I can easily admit making mistakes.	_____	_____	_____
4. When asked to do a job I dislike, I can express my feelings about the job.	_____	_____	_____
5. I believe I have the ability to accomplish most tasks that I begin.	_____	_____	_____
6. I do not have a difficult time telling others no.	_____	_____	_____
7. I do not mind being watched when I work.	_____	_____	_____
8. Eye contact is important when talking, and I try to maintain it.	_____	_____	_____
9. When I get mad, I try not to show feelings through anger, frustration, or disappointment.	_____	_____	_____
10. I believe that what I want or need is as important as the wants and needs of others.	_____	_____	_____
11. If someone is demonstrating an irritating habit, I feel free to ask the person to stop.	_____	_____	_____
12. I can deal with conflict in an adult manner.	_____	_____	_____
13. When someone shoves in front of me, I usually call their attention to it.	_____	_____	_____
14. When someone criticizes me, I try to learn from it.	_____	_____	_____
15. When I don't agree with a person, I can gently express my disagreement.	_____	_____	_____

	Almost Always	Sometimes	Almost Never
16. I feel I am not always right about everything.	_____	_____	_____
17. I do not mind asking my friends for small favors.	_____	_____	_____
18. In social situations, I prefer to be in the background rather than in the limelight.	_____	_____	_____

1 | Why Is Assertive Behavior Important?

This chapter will help you to:

- See the difference between assertive behavior and aggressive or nonassertive behavior.
- Identify when assertive behavior could be important to you.

Most people at one time or another have been made to feel uncomfortable with those around them. Do you often feel you are not included, put down, betrayed, or used? Do you want to speak up for yourself but, instead, think, "I just can't say anything. I don't want to embarrass myself or look foolish," or, "I wish I knew how to express my feelings." Or do you speak up and express yourself in ways that are interpreted as being aggressive?

Both nonassertive and aggressive behavior keep you from being direct and honest in your interaction with others. In assertive behavior, your goal is to increase your ability to manage your interaction with others positively. You should be honest and direct to fulfill your needs, wants, or desires, and do so without hurting others.

Whether you want to improve your assertive skills or help others improve their skills, reading this book is the first step toward learning more about assertiveness.

Take the place and attitude to which you see your unquestionable right, and all men acquiesce.

—Ralph Waldo Emerson

THE IMPACT OF ASSERTIVE BEHAVIOR

Assertive behavior is important because when you act assertively you:

- Gain self-esteem by expressing yourself in an honest, straightforward manner.
- Gain confidence by experiencing success at being assertive.
- Are able to stand up for yourself when you need to.
- Can negotiate productively with others.
- Promote your personal growth and fulfillment.
- Adopt a self-managed life-style of your wants, needs, and desires.
- Take responsibility for the quality of relationships with others.

Being assertive means taking risks, such as speaking honestly about how you think and feel, and expressing what your desires, needs, and wants are, while considering the feelings of others. Learning to act assertively allows *you*—not other people—to manage your wants, needs, and desires. You may not always get what you want, but having the courage to speak up will cause you to feel better about yourself. In the process, you become a happier, more fulfilled person.

Your Turn

Describe why assertive behavior would be important to you or your work group in the following situations. We've completed this exercise in the model below.

Model: A co-worker asks you to help complete a project that is not your responsibility, and you know the co-worker has plenty of time but has waited until the last minute to start work.

Benefits of assertiveness

1. *You may not have to do the work if you speak up.*
2. *The co-worker learns that you will not do his or her work, so he or she won't ask in the future.*
3. *You gain confidence.*
4. *You gain self-esteem.*

Situation 1:   There is an unpleasant job that has to be done, and you have been asked to do it.

Benefits of assertiveness

1. _____
   _____
2. _____
   _____
3. _____
   _____
4. _____
   _____
5. _____
   _____

Situation 2: The supervisor criticizes you unfairly.

Benefits of assertiveness

1. _____
   _____
2. _____
   _____
3. _____
   _____
4. _____
   _____
5. _____
   _____

Situation 3: An employee or co-worker isn't doing his or her job, and it is your responsibility to see that the co-worker does it.

Benefits of assertiveness

1. _____
   _____
2. _____
   _____
3. _____
   _____
4. _____
   _____
5. _____
   _____

Situation 4: Your supervisor rejects your excellent idea that could save time and money.

Benefits of assertiveness

1. _____
   _____
2. _____
   _____
3. _____
   _____

4. _____

_____

5. _____

_____

Situation 5: A co-worker constantly asks you for favors you do not want to do.

Benefits of assertiveness

1. _____

_____

2. _____

_____

3. _____

_____

4. _____

_____

5. _____

_____

All things are difficult before they are easy.

—John Norley

Chapter Checkpoints

Assertive behavior is important because you:

✓ Gain self-esteem and confidence in expressing yourself.

✓ Can negotiate productively with others.

✓ Can change negative work situations into positive ones.

✓ Use it to strengthen relationships at work.

2 Assertive, Aggressive, and Nonassertive Behaviors

This chapter will help you to:

- Recognize assertive, aggressive, and nonassertive behaviors.
- Determine when and where it is appropriate to use assertive behavior.

In any work situation, you have a choice to be assertive, aggressive, or nonassertive. Your choice depends on many factors, of course, but it is almost always best to choose assertive behavior.

When making a decision, for instance, you have three options:

- If you make decisions based on information and your needs, *you are acting assertively.*
- If you make decisions based on their potential for influencing others or with no regard to their impact on others, *you are acting aggressively.*
- If you leave decisions to others or make decisions to avoid conflict, *you are acting nonassertively.*

The first option, of course, is the one that will be the most satisfying.

WHAT IS ASSERTIVE BEHAVIOR?

Behaving assertively allows you to express your needs, thoughts, and feelings honestly and directly without violating the rights of others. Acting assertively enables you to:

1. Make your own decisions about careers, relationships, and life-styles.
2. Set limits on your time and energy.
3. Express agreement or disagreement.
4. Respond to violations of your rights or those of others.

In short, assertive behavior focuses on solving interpersonal problems through straightforward action.

WHAT IS AGGRESSIVE BEHAVIOR?

Aggressive behavior should not be confused with assertive behavior. When you express your needs, thoughts, and feelings in ways that humiliate or dominate others or that ignore the rights of others, you are acting aggressively. True, you are expressing your desires and feelings—but in a negative or hostile manner. For instance, if you have a manipulative leadership style, you are acting aggressively in an indirect way. As a result, your colleagues might respond with confusion, distrust, or resentment. Aggressive behavior aims at hurting or dominating another person, physically or emotionally. In other words, the aggressive person always aims to win over the other person in a conflict.

WHAT IS NONASSERTIVE BEHAVIOR?

When you act nonassertively or passively, you do not express your own needs, thoughts, and feelings. In fact, you ignore yourself in such a way as to allow others to force their wants and desires on you. Nonassertive or passive behavior inhibits you from expressing yourself honestly and directly. It can cause you to build up anger and to feel negative about yourself. Why? Because you are not getting what you want or achieving your goals. You may feel you are being treated badly, yet cannot do anything about it.

As you continue to act nonassertively, your negative experiences tend to tear down your confidence and self-esteem, so you lose self-respect. If you are nonassertive at work, your managers or supervisors may ignore or overrule you. Your co-workers may respond to you with frustration and anger because they do not understand why you let others make decisions and avoid open conflict.

> There are three possible broad approaches to the conduct of interpersonal relations. The first is to consider one's self only and ride roughshod over others. . . . The second . . . is always to put others before oneself. . . . The third approach is the golden mean. . . . The individual places himself first, but takes others into account.
>
> —Joseph Wolpe

COMPARING THE STYLES

The way a person handles a particular situation distinguishes his or her behavior as assertive, aggressive, or nonassertive. Here are several approaches to handling a typical work conflict.

Your manager calls you on Monday morning and tells you that your project is being hampered by problems from another department. Your manager needs to talk with you about it sometime today when there is more time. You say:

A. "I'd like you to be more specific with me. Let's decide on a time when we can get together and talk." You *want* to know specifics and you *feel* comfortable about asking for a specific time in an adult manner. (Assertive)

2

B. "Well, we're near completion! How many more times are we going to have to deal with problems from that department? We're going to have to get them to change. . . ." You are angry and frustrated. (Aggressive)

C. "Okay." When you hang up the telephone, you feel it's **not** okay. You are left anxious and confused, not knowing what the conference with your manager will cover, or even when it will occur. Now you wish you had asked for more information. Why didn't you? (Nonassertive)

Success is a journey not a destination.

—Ben Sweetland

Your Turn

Match the statements in Column A with the appropriate behavior style in Column B. Place the appropriate alphabetic character in the space provided.

2

	Column A	Column B
_____	1. "Well, I'm not sure. It's hard for me to decide."	A. Assertive
_____	2. "How stupid can you be?"	B. Aggressive
_____	3. "I hate to ask you, but . . . ."	C. Nonassertive
_____	4. "I can't do that! I've got more work than I can do already. I don't have time for you right now!"	
_____	5. "Sure, I'd like to do that."	
_____	6. "I really don't want to but because you asked me to . . . ."	
_____	7. "Uh, I was wondering, would you be willing to take the time to help me?"	
_____	8. "It's your fault that we are not getting the funds we needed."	
_____	9. "No, thank you. I do appreciate your inviting me."	
_____	10. "Because I am in charge, there isn't a darn thing you can do about it."	

Compare your answers with those on the next page.

2

ANSWERS

1. C—Hesitant; shows lack of confidence.
2. B—Harsh, blameful; encourages resentment and defensiveness.
3. C—Timid, apologetic, defensive; invites disregard.
4. B—Disrespectful, abrupt; invites humiliation.
5. A—Genuine; shows decisiveness and cooperation.
6. C—Passive; leaves decision to others.
7. C—Timid, passive; invites disregard to request.
8. B—Blameful; fosters defensiveness.
9. A—Direct; invites respect.
10. B—Controlling, dominant; invites resentment.

Your Turn

List five statements you have either said to yourself or have heard others say that would indicate assertive, aggressive, or nonassertive behavior style. After you list a statement, use these abbreviations to identify it: AS (Assertive); AG (Aggressive); NS (Nonassertive).

1. _____
   _____

2. _____
   _____

3. _____
   _____

4. _____
   _____

5. _____
   _____

Your Turn

Describe a situation in which you have observed someone who has acted assertively, another situation in which someone acted aggressively, and a third situation in which someone acted nonassertively.

2

Situation 1: Assertive behavior

What were the main characteristics of the behavior?

_____

_____

Which of these characteristics is the most important?

_____

_____

Of all the characteristics you identified, which of these is dominant?

_____

_____

Situation 2: Aggressive behavior

What were the main characteristics of the behavior?

_____

_____

Of all the characteristics you identified, which of these is dominant?

_____

_____

Which needs improvement?

_____

_____

Situation 3: Nonassertive behavior

What were the main characteristics of the behavior?

_____

_____

Of all the characteristics you identified, which of these is dominant?

_____

_____

Which needs improvement?

_____

_____

The basic message in . . .

Assertion is: This is what I think; this is what I feel; and this is what I want.

Aggression is: This is what I think—you're absurd for thinking differently; this is what I feel—your feelings don't count; and this is what I want—what you want isn't important.

Nonassertion is: Whatever I think is not important to you; what I feel doesn't matter; and what I want doesn't count.

Chapter Checkpoints

Being assertive allows you to:

✓ Ask for what you want.

✓ Not feel guilty.

✓ Not be pushed around by others.

✓ Respect individuality.

✓ Be flexible.

✓ Admit mistakes.

✓ Take responsibility.

✓ Let others know of your expectations.

✓ State your views.

3 | Obstacles to Acting Assertively

This chapter will help you to:

- Recognize three common obstacles to acting assertively.
- Identify situations where obstacles keep *you* from acting assertively.

Why is a person more comfortable in certain situations than in others? In any given situation, one person may act assertively without any difficulty, while another person may have difficulty acting assertively. Three common obstacles to assertiveness are low self-esteem, inability to handle conflict, and poor communication. Identifying these obstacles may increase your opportunities to overcome them and act assertively.

OBSTACLE #1:   LOW SELF-ESTEEM

There is a difference between self-esteem and self-concept. Self-esteem is self-respect. Self-concept is the mental picture you have of your strengths, weaknesses, successes, and failures. Self-concept, of course, is a major factor in self-esteem. Your self-concept influences your goals, temperament, and actions. If you view yourself as result-oriented, organized, and disciplined, you may see yourself as a person who can accomplish goals. Most likely you have high self-esteem. On the other hand, if you see yourself as insecure, limited in your skills and abilities, or prone to fly off the handle, then you may see yourself as inadequate, and probably have low self-esteem. When you have a good mental picture of yourself, you build positive self-esteem, then act accordingly.

Self-Concept   →   Self-Esteem   →   Positive Behavior

Whether or not you are assertive depends on your self-esteem. Individuals who act nonassertively or aggressively in situations do so because they replay situations when they failed or they felt anxious.

A nonassertive person with low self-esteem would probably enact the following scene:

Johanna wants to apply for a promotion within her company. So far, she has acted nonassertively because she recalls a past situation when she applied for a promotion and did not receive it. Because of her low self-esteem, she begins to think negatively about herself and does not apply for the job. After someone else in her department receives the promotion, Johanna copes by becoming very tense, forming negative mental images of herself, and telling herself, "I have failed. I wouldn't have gotten the job anyway. It is a good thing I didn't apply." Johanna is in a vicious cycle—each nonassertive situation with its negative mental images continues to feed her low self-esteem.

An aggressive person with low self-esteem would handle another situation this way:

Grant is in a meeting with several managers discussing requests for additional personnel. He believes this is a waste of time because he's already made several requests, and has been denied. In the meeting, he openly attacks the personnel director in front of the general manager and gets into an argument with him about his negative, aggressive attitude. The personnel manager ends the discussion, but Grant wants to continue arguing. He ends up storming out of the meeting. After cooling off and thinking through what happened, he begins to think: "I shouldn't have blown up like that! I don't know what gets into me; and with the general manager there! If I'm not careful, I'll lose my job." Grant becomes more aggressive as he becomes more frustrated when situations are repeatedly unresolved.

No one can make you feel inferior without your consent.
—Eleanor Roosevelt

People who are always nonassertive or aggressive can limit themselves in many ways particularly by denying themselves opportunities for career growth and advancement.

Your Turn

Describe a work situation when you did not assert yourself because it reminded you of a previous failure.

_____

_____

_____

_____

_____

3

What Are You Telling Yourself?

We become what we habitually contemplate.

—George Russell

Not only do people talk to others, but they talk to themselves. People are greatly influenced by their self-talk. At times, everyone thinks negative thoughts, but continued negative self-talk lowers the individual's self-esteem. Steps leading to your negative self-talk may follow this pattern:

1. As a situation occurs, you compare the circumstances to past experiences.

2. Because your past experiences have been negative in some way, you choose not to assert yourself in the present situation.

3. After the situation is over, you feel you should have responded assertively rather than nonassertively or aggressively. If you are nonassertive you might ask, "Why didn't I?" If you are aggressive, you may condemn yourself for losing control, or might confuse your aggression for assertion.

4. As a nonassertive person, you realize that you did not act assertively because you did not want to experience the feeling of anxiety or failure again. If you are aggressive, you may feel the same way, if you got past Step 3.

5. Because you are anxious, worried, and nervous in this situation, you begin to feel badly about not asserting yourself. You start telling yourself, "I am incapable," "I won't be able to," and so forth. You get on the low self-esteem treadmill.

Your Turn

Using the situation you described in the previous Your Turn activity, analyze the steps you went through that led up to negative self-talk. Complete the following numbered items.

1. What past negative experience(s) prevented you from asserting yourself?

   _____

   _____

   _____

2. Describe the following actions or reactions you had concerning the negative results of those experiences.

   a. Outward actions, such as:

   _____

   b. Negative images, such as:

   _____

3. What negative statements did you tell yourself?

   _____
   _____
   _____

OBSTACLE #2: INABILITY TO HANDLE CONFLICT

When you act assertively in a conflict situation, you leave the communication line open for dialogue long after the conflict is resolved. People who fear conflict avoid asserting themselves in stressful situations.

What Is Your Attitude toward Conflict?

Your attitude toward conflict results from how you were taught to deal with conflict as a child and how you have learned to deal with conflict with your peers, friends, and family members as an adult. If you have been able to resolve conflict successfully throughout your life, you probably developed a positive attitude toward conflict. But if your experiences were negative, you may have learned to act nonassertively or aggressively.

Your Turn

Write your responses to the following questions in the space provided.

1. As a child, how were you taught to deal with conflict?

   _____
   _____
   _____

2. As an adult, how have you learned to deal with conflict?

_____

_____

_____

OBSTACLE #3:
POOR COMMUNICATION SKILLS

Few people are trained in assertive communication skills, such as defending themselves against aggressive verbal put-downs. The inability to respond can create a buildup of resentment, anxiety, and other negative emotions. In order to head them off, you need to learn to express yourself directly and clearly. Knowing how to respond to put-downs, compliments, generalizations, and body language can enhance your relationships with others. Have you ever walked away from a situation and said to yourself, "Why didn't I think of anything to say?"

Your Turn

Think of two put-downs that you wished you had responded to assertively. Write the statement and your response in the space provided.

1. Statement:

_____

_____

Your response:

_____

_____

2. Statement:

_____

_____

Your response:

_____

_____

Chapter Checkpoints

Three obstacles to assertiveness:

Obstacle #1:   Low Self-Esteem

✓ Self-concept (your mental image of yourself) builds self-esteem (self-respect), which determines your behavior.

✓ Negative thinking and actions may limit your opportunities.

Obstacle #2:   Inability to Handle Conflict

✓ People who fear conflict avoid asserting themselves in stressful situations.

✓ Do not mistake aggressive behavior for assertive behavior— aggressive behavior causes conflict.

Obstacle #3:   Poor Communication Skills

✓ Your inability to respond in various situations leads to negative emotions, thoughts, and anxiety.

4 | Improving Your Self-Esteem

This chapter will help you to:

- Identify the two major sources of self-esteem.
- Practice changing your negative self-statements to positive self-statements.

In this chapter, you will find out how to improve your self-esteem through a better understanding of it. There are common obstacles that tend to keep people from acting assertively. The first of these obstacles is low self-esteem. Your thoughts and feelings, either positive or negative, can affect your assertiveness.

As we saw in Chapter 3, people who are assertive tend to have positive self-esteem while nonassertive and aggressive people tend to have low self-esteem.

Thinking negative thoughts and experiencing negative feelings about yourself contributes to low self-esteem. Suppose you made this self-defeating statement in an interview: "You may not want to hire me because I don't have much experience." A negative statement such as this might cause you to seem unconfident in your abilities even though you really are highly capable! Don't let negative thoughts about yourself hold you back or keep you from getting what you want and deserve.

You must also keep in mind that your level of self-esteem can change. Just because your self-esteem is negative doesn't mean it will always remain so, and the reverse is also true. Low self-esteem doesn't have to last forever. A series of successes can improve self-esteem and cause you to be more assertive. Likewise, a series of failures can damage positive self-esteem, and suddenly you become insecure and more nonassertive or aggressive. The good news is that low self-esteem can be transformed into positive self-esteem!

It is difficult to make a man miserable while he feels worthy of himself and claims kindred to the great God who made him.

—Abraham Lincoln

SOURCES OF SELF-ESTEEM

Your self-esteem comes from two sources.

What other people tell you about yourself—how well you have done or how badly you have done.

Self-observation of your own behavior and its consequences—how well you perform builds your self-confidence.

What Other People Tell You

From birth onward, others have been observing you and telling you about yourself. As a child, you relied upon your mother, father, teachers, church leaders, police, and other authorities to tell you if your actions were appropriate. As an adult, you are judged by your peers on how you behave according to certain accepted standards. If your experiences have been positive, you have probably developed positive self-esteem. If your experiences have been negative, you may have developed a feeling of failure, resulting in low self-esteem.

Positive Self-Esteem:

Praise from parents over grades in school.

Praise from teachers over excellent work.

Recognition through awards.

Good job performance evaluations.

Praise for performing your job as required.

Low Self-Esteem

Lack of praise for grades, leaving you feeling unable to measure up to others' standards.

Statements made by teachers, making you feel you were not capable.

Statements from a peer about the quality of your work.

Low expectations from a supervisor.

No praise, even though you are doing your job well.

Y o u r   T u r n

1. Identify a positive experience from childhood, in which you were measured by your intelligence, your manners, or how well you played with other children. How did this experience build positive self-esteem?

   _____

   _____

   _____

   _____

2. Identify a situation from adulthood, in which a peer measured, labeled, or judged you according to a standard, causing you to have positive thoughts or feelings.

   _____

   _____

   _____

> People forget how fast you did a job—but they remember how well you did it.
> —Howard W. Newton

Observing Your Behavior and Its Consequences

The second source of self-esteem is observation of your own behavior and its consequences. As you move through life you begin to think, feel, and talk to yourself in a certain way about those experiences. You give yourself either positive or negative strokes for each experience.

Suppose you had the responsibility of firing someone and it resulted in a bad experience for you. You may feel anxiety resulting from self-defeating thoughts the next time you face a similar situation. Because of these self-defeating thoughts, you may become more nonassertive or aggressive in the next situation. The reverse is true as well. If you had a good experience and, therefore, had positive thoughts about your skill in accomplishing a difficult task, you may become more assertive in future similar situations.

Y o u r   T u r n

Identify a situation in which a peer measured, labeled, or judged you according to a standard, causing you to have negative thoughts or feelings.

_____

_____

_____

4

A great pleasure in life is doing what people say you cannot do.

—Walt Gagehot

Change Your Prophecy

At the heart of low self-esteem is the concept of the **self-fulfilling prophecy**—whatever you expect to happen will happen. Your expectations, negative or positive, are fulfilled. If you anticipate problems, they often occur. If you anticipate smooth sailing, you will increase the chance of a positive outcome.

How is the self-fulfilling prophecy related to assertiveness? If you have low self-esteem and say "I can't," you send messages to others that you are going to fail. You are then treated as if you will fail. You set yourself up for failure before you begin! On the other hand, if you have positive self-esteem and say "I can," you are viewed as if you will succeed.

Your Turn

Identify a situation in which you experienced the self-fulfilling prophecy.

_____
_____
_____
_____
_____

DEVELOPING YOUR OWN ASSERTIVE OUTLOOK

When you adopt an assertive attitude, you can develop your own assertive outlook through practice and repetition. Develop your own assertive outlook using the sample on page 29 as a model. Remember that by building this outlook into your positive self-talk (see Chapter 3), you'll change the way you see yourself.

MY ASSERTIVE OUTLOOK

1. I accept each person as he or she is.
2. I can never change another person.
3. I accept that each person communicates differently based on his or her values, background, and environment.
4. I accept responsibility for myself and not for others.
5. I am responsible only for my side of a relationship.
6. I accept that every person may choose to be assertive, nonassertive, or aggressive.
7. I have a choice of being assertive, nonassertive, or aggressive depending on the situation.

8. I will practice being assertive, being sensitive to the feelings of others.

Can you add to your assertive outlook?

9. _____
   _____

10. _____
   _____

CHANGING YOUR NEGATIVE SELF-STATEMENTS

To become assertive, you must have positive self-esteem and believe you can act effectively. Here are two ways you can improve your self-esteem.

Increase the frequency of positive self-statements and reward yourself for doing so.	Decrease how often you describe your weaknesses, and refrain from dwelling on negative thoughts.

The positive self-statements may not necessarily be true at the time you are saying them to yourself, but should reflect the *goal* that you want to attain. In other words, you might be well-organized part of the time, but your goal is to stay organized all the time. If you said a negative self-statement such as "I hate to take time to get organized," you might be prone to putting off the time necessary to achieve the goal. On the other hand, if you make a positive self-statement such as "I can organize my work quickly and easily," just the fact that you are bringing the idea to mind helps you focus on your goal.

Your Turn

List three positive self-statements that you want to say more often. For instance:

I can learn new concepts quickly.

I play golf well.

1. _____

2. _____

3. _____

List a way you might reward yourself for thinking or feeling each of the positive thoughts listed above. For instance:

I will buy myself the new book _____ I have been wanting.

I will attend the movie entitled _____.

1. _____

2. _____

3. _____

Target any specific negative self-statements you want to avoid by listing them here:

1. _____

2. _____

3. _____

List ways you might "punish" yourself when you realize you have been dwelling on negative thoughts and feelings. For instance:

I will not have dessert with lunch.

I will mow the lawn as soon as I get home today.

I will clean the garage (or closet).

1. _____

2. _____

3. _____

We are continually faced by great opportunities brilliantly disguised as insoluble problems.

—Author Unknown

You have the right to express your thoughts and feelings and to make positive and negative statements to yourself. In order to change the habit of making negative self-statements, you must revise your mental image. Practice is the key.

4

Here are some tips for revising your mental image and taking positive steps toward self-esteem.

- Share your desire to change with a peer, friend, or family member.
- Set a goal realistic to reach: for instance, make a concentrated effort to say only positive statements to yourself no matter what the situation in one day.
- Share your successes as well as failures with a peer, friend, or family member.
- Keep a record of positive thoughts. Place them on note cards or post notes and place them where you can refer to them often.
- "Punish" yourself for dwelling on your negative self-thoughts with an undesirable activity such as filing, cleaning a closet, or trimming the shrubbery.

ASSERTIVENESS RIGHTS

You have probably heard of the slogan "Stand up for yourself" or "Stand up for your rights." You may have viewed these statements in a negative way, saying, "Don't be pushy" or "Don't take advantage of others." This way of thinking may have kept you from becoming aware of your rights and standing up for them. The central theme of assertive behavior is that you know your rights and feel good about expressing them by using the techniques in this book. The list below suggests rights for you to consider in developing your assertive behavior.

I have the right to:

1. Be treated with respect.
2. Be appreciated.
3. Express my feelings (in an honest, direct, and appropriate manner, not as a device for attack).
4. Disagree and to express my opinions (in a way that will lead to resolution of conflict).
5. Set my own priorities.
6. Say no without feeling guilty.
7. Express my needs and wants.
8. Make mistakes (and be responsible for them).

9. Choose not to assert myself in any situation. (In some cases, it may be better to *choose* to be nonassertive.)

10. Make my own decisions.

Your Turn

Change the following negative self-statements to positive self-statements.

1. "I can't do that."

   _____

2. "I can't express my opinion."

   _____

3. "I can't ask for help."

   _____

4. "I don't have a lot of confidence in myself."

   _____

5. "It seems as if I always make mistakes."

   _____

6. Others:

   _____
   _____
   _____
   _____
   _____
   _____

4

Your Turn

How Well Did You Do?

Here is a follow-up form to assess your progress on making positive self-statements and rewarding or punishing yourself as needed. Complete one line for each positive self-statement you are working on.

Positive Self-Statement	Person Shared With	Date	Succeeded Y (Yes) N (No)	Try Again Date	Rewards/ Punishments
1.					
2.					
3.					
4.					
5.					
6.					
7.					
8.					
9.					
10.					

Chapter Checkpoints

✓ Constant negative thoughts and negative feelings about yourself contribute to low self-esteem.

✓ Self-esteem can be changed from negative to positive.

✓ Your self-esteem is derived from what other people tell you about yourself and what you observe about your own behavior and its consequences.

✓ You *can* change your negative self-statements into positive ones.

5 | Handling Conflict

This chapter will help you to:

- Identify irrational beliefs that keep you from asserting yourself.
- Compare assertive behavior with aggressive and nonassertive behaviors in handling conflict.
- Learn guidelines for resolving conflict.

IRRATIONAL BELIEFS

If assertive behavior is an expression of your thoughts, feelings, and needs in a direct and positive way, then why should assertiveness be a problem? When you are faced with conflict, your thoughts, beliefs, attitudes, and feelings set the stage for your behavior.

Your mind needs to be free to respond to each new situation calling for assertive action. Irrational attitudes, beliefs, and thoughts hold back and inhibit people. They keep a person from behaving as assertively as he or she would like. Here is an example of irrational thinking:

Florina:

"You had some very good ideas about the topics for the upcoming conference. Why didn't you express your ideas in the planning session?"

Ching Lee:

"If I had expressed my ideas in the meeting with that group, they would have challenged me. Now I wish I had shared my ideas."

In this situation, Ching Lee's irrational thinking distorted reality by focusing on and anticipating the worst possible outcome (his ideas would be challenged) if he had asserted himself. When a person adopts irrational thinking, he or she is overly concerned with how he or she thinks others will react and ends up not being assertive. Even though Florina recognized Ching's good ideas, Ching focused on his negative thinking and ignored all the positive outcomes, such as speaking up and possibly gaining respect, that might have resulted from his assertiveness in the meeting.

Focus on Rational Thinking

You can become more successful in asserting yourself if you change your irrational beliefs and replace them with rational ones. Rational thinking includes understanding that there are many possible outcomes to any assertive action. In other words, even if you assert yourself and the result is negative, you learn that you can handle the situation by choosing not to be devastated by it.

Here is a rational thought to replace Ching's irrational one: "Even if I expressed my ideas about the conference topics and they were not accepted, it's all right. I did express myself even if the others do not accept my ideas at this time." Subscribing to irrational thoughts can prevent you from asserting yourself in any given situation.

Face Conflict

Avoiding conflict is also an obstacle to assertive behavior. Recall how you were taught to deal with conflict as a child and how you have learned to deal with conflict as an adult. (Review your responses in Chapter 2.) If you have adopted irrational beliefs relating to conflict, you may not assert yourself in conflict situations.

You may believe that if you assert yourself in a conflict, others will be angry at you. You can replace this irrational belief with a rational one—you do not have to feel responsible for another person's anger. If that person becomes angry, it is his or her problem. Once you recognize your irrational belief and try to replace it with a rational one, you will feel more comfortable about asserting yourself in conflict.

Your Turn

List some irrational beliefs that have led you to avoid conflict. For example, "If I assert myself in conflict, *I will be criticized*." Complete the following statements.

1. If I assert myself in conflict,

_____

2. If I assert myself in conflict,

_____

3. If I assert myself in conflict,

_____

Check your answers with the suggested responses on the next page.

SUGGESTED RESPONSES

"If I assert myself in conflict, I will not be liked or accepted."

"If I assert myself in conflict, others will get mad."

"If I assert myself in conflict, others will get their feelings hurt."

"If I assert myself in conflict, I don't think he or she could handle it."

For every minute you remain angry, you give up sixty seconds of peace of mind.

—Ralph Waldo Emerson

Your Turn

Replace the irrational beliefs in the last exercise by rational statements below. Remember that most irrational beliefs stem from an unrealistic view of a situation and its consequences.

1. _____

2. _____

3. _____

DIFFERENT BEHAVIOR STYLES FOR HANDLING CONFLICT

If you are not using assertive behavior in situations where you have to deal with confrontation or disagreement, you may be choosing another behavior—aggressive or nonassertive. How do these behaviors address conflict?

Assertive Behavior

- Brings conflict into the open where the communication process can continue.
- Is interested in a "win-win" situation; understands that it's okay to get angry but in a way that expresses feeling.
- Tries to negotiate to solve problems in an environment of mutual respect.
- Recognizes personal rights while respecting the rights of others.
- Uses statements such as "This is how I see it," "This is how I feel," or "This is what I think."

Aggressive Behavior

- Becomes defensive.
- Discounts feelings of others; assumes an "I'm right" position.
- Is interested in a "win" situation at the expense of the relationship.
- Uses anger to control.
- Tries to manipulate.
- Uses statements such as "The meeting is at 2 P.M.; I don't care what you have on your schedule; just be here."

Nonassertive Behavior

- Gives in to others' expectations and viewpoints to avoid conflict.
- Assumes a "You're right" position; doesn't see personal feelings as important.
- Will end up in a "lose" situation.
- Is easily manipulated by an aggressive person.
- Does not openly show anger.
- Uses statements such as "How can I possibly know the answer to that?"

For most people, the three behavior types are seen in the following terms:

1. *Assertive:* Direct, firm, honest, tactful; makes things happen, maintains self-respect and gains respect from others; confident, positive.
2. *Aggressive:* Domineering, forceful, bold; makes things happen regardless of how others feel or think; mean, uncaring, forward, pushy, belligerent.
3. *Nonassertive:* Soft-hearted, modest, hesitant, insecure, withdrawn; waits to make things happen; loses self-respect because things never quite happen according to plan.

5

Y o u r   T u r n

Now think of a situation where there is conflict.

1. Describe the situation.

   _____
   _____
   _____

2. Identify any irrational beliefs that may keep you from asserting your-self in the situation you've described above.

   _____
   _____
   _____

3. Choose words to identify your behavior (assertive, aggressive, and nonassertive) in handling the conflict in Step 1.

   _____
   _____
   _____

HOW CAN WE IMPROVE THE PROCESS OF RESOLVING CONFLICT?

In any conflict, you can choose to work for mutual understanding and agreement. Or, you could defend your position aggressively or nonasser-tively. If you handle conflict by exploring your real feelings, thoughts, and desires to solve problems, you focus on the issues and the process, rather than on lack of confidence or self-doubt. You build your confidence and increase your self-esteem.

By handling conflict in this way, you build mutual respect with your co-workers and supervisor. You become more creative in initiating activities that will help you work through difficulties with others. You increase your chances of solving the underlying problem that would otherwise erupt into additional conflicts at a later time.

Conflict is more easily resolved when you:

- Avoid personal attacks and stick to the issues.
- Act honestly and directly toward others.

- Emphasize points of agreement as a foundation for discussion of points of argument.
- Avoid a "win-lose" position; remain flexible.
- Seek solutions rather than placing blame.
- Agree upon some means of negotiation or exchange.

Your Turn

Place a checkmark beside each statement that improves the chances of resolving conflict assertively.

_____ 1. "You are the cause of all our problems in this office."

_____ 2. "I really prefer not working with you."

_____ 3. "I understand how you feel, but the statement you made about our procedures for ordering supplies only increased Joe's anxiety."

_____ 4. "I see we agree on the first three points in the contract. Now let's take a look at the remaining point and see how we may resolve our differences."

_____ 5. "We must follow the regulations to the letter. There are no shades of gray."

_____ 6. "Carlos, I understand how you feel about the changes you are suggesting; but because of our limited time, let's continue as we are for the next two months. At the end of two months, let's reevaluate our plan."

Compare your responses to those given below.

SELECTED SUGGESTED RESPONSES

3. Expresses an understanding of the other person's feelings; explains the specific statement that increased Joe's anxiety. Does not verbally attack anyone.

4. Points of agreement were emphasized in order to move the points of potential argument.

6. Expresses an understanding of the other person's feelings; sets up a situation in which negotiations could begin.

One man with courage makes a majority.

—Andrew Jackson

Chapter Checkpoints

To assert yourself in conflict:

✓ Identify irrational beliefs that keep you from asserting yourself.

✓ Replace irrational beliefs with rational ones that help you assert yourself.

✓ Respond by behaving assertively.

✓ Follow general guidelines to resolve conflict more easily:
- Avoid personal attacks and stick to the issues.
- Act honestly and directly toward others.
- Emphasize points of agreement as a foundation for discussion of points of argument.
- Avoid a "win-lose" position; remain flexible.
- Seek solutions rather than deciding who is to blame.
- Agree upon some means of negotiation or exchange.

6 | Using I-Statements

This chapter will help you to:

- Use I-statements.
- Become a better communicator.

Very few people succeed without being clear about their own goals and objectives or without standing up for themselves. Clear communication is a big part of assertiveness.

Consider your following encounter with Rosita: "*You* told me you would be here at 8 A.M. It is now 8:30! Where in the *?!* have you been? *You* never can keep an appointment." You are offended by her direct attack and want to tell her so. But most people find that if they try to tell someone how they really feel at the moment, both of them end up getting upset. If you were to tell Rosita how you felt about her attack, then she might feel defensive, even though there was a misunderstanding about the appointment. No wonder people tend not to tell one another how they feel about what was said. The more negative experiences you have like this, the more likely you are to behave nonassertively or aggressively.

WHAT IS AN I-STATEMENT?

An effective assertive communication technique is to:

- Use I-statements rather than you-statements.

Here is an example of an aggressive you-statement:

Maria:
"*You* think Bryan can do a better job than I can on the Harper report."

An aggressive statement like this one usually puts the other person on the defensive. Why? Because it began with *you*, and the word *you* can be perceived as an attack. When a person starts the sentence with *you* in a stressful situation, the voice is often louder, intensifying the situation.

Here is an example of an assertive I-statement:

Maria:

> "I get angry when you ask Bryan to work on the Harper report. I'd like you to come to me next time you want the report worked on because it is my responsibility."

This time, Maria began with I. She expressed her feelings (anger), described the behavior (you ask Bryan to work on the Harper report), identified the outcome (she wants you to come to her next time instead of to Bryan), and explained why (because it is her responsibility).

HOW TO CREATE I-STATEMENTS

I-statements can be created in four steps:

1. Begin with the word *I*.
2. Express what you feel, think, or need:

   I feel anger . . .

   I think this because . . .

   I need this to be done because . . .
3. Describe the other person's behavior that created the situation.
4. Express the outcome or change you desire and why you need it.

I-statements help you:

- Take responsibility for your thoughts, feelings, wants, and needs.
- Avoid blaming anyone for a situation or conflict.
- Tell the other person what you honestly think, feel, want, or need.

When you can comfortably use I-statements, you will:

- Decrease the chance of being misunderstood.
- Feel better about expressing your feelings, wants, and needs.

- See improvement in your relationships.
- Increase your confidence and improve your self-esteem.
- Avoid a high emotional level of behavior.
- Have an objective formula to use in times of stress.

6

Your Turn

Identify each of the parts of the I-statement by writing your answers in the blanks provided.

Example: "I feel my workload is too heavy because I need to work a lot of overtime to get everything done. I'd like to talk to you about some possible solutions because I want to be able to do a good job."

Part I (I-statement):

  I . . .
_____

Part II (describe how you feel, think, or what you need):

  . . . feel my workload is too heavy.
_____

Part III (other person's behavior):

  . . . because you have assigned me lots of work or it has simply

  evolved.
_____

Part IV (desired outcome):

  I'd like to talk to you about some possible solutions so I can do

  a good job.
_____

1. "I get irritated when you interrupt me when I am talking. I'd like to finish what I have to say before you speak because I lose my train of thought."

   Part I: _____
   Part II: _____
   Part III: _____
   Part IV: _____

2. "I get angry when you tell me you will support me, and then don't support me in a meeting. In the future, I want to be able to count on your support. We *can* get the proposal approved if we show cooperation."

   Part I: _____
   Part II: _____
   Part III: _____
   Part IV: _____

3. "I think the decisions made by the committee should be followed. I feel anxious when I don't apply the rules they have set. In the future, I want to go strictly by the committee's decisions because those were our instructions."

Part I: _____
Part II: _____
Part III: _____
Part IV: _____

4. "I understand that there are times when you must be absent; and lately you have been absent once a week for the past three weeks. In the future, I need you here because the work of other people is delayed when you aren't here to do your part."

Part I: _____
Part II: _____
Part III: _____
Part IV: _____

Read the following statements, add any information necessary, and in the space provided change the *you* statements to I-statements.

5. "You are always late for our meetings."

_____
_____

6. "You never return phone calls."

_____
_____

7. "When you don't do your job, I have to do it for you."

_____
_____

8. "You don't meet deadlines."

_____
_____

Compare your answers with those on the next page.

SUGGESTED RESPONSES

6

1. Part I:　I
   Part II:　get irritated
   Part III:　when you interrupt me when I am talking.
   Part IV:　I'd like to finish what I have to say before you speak because I lose my train of thought.

2. Part I:　I
   Part II:　get angry
   Part III:　when you tell me you will support me and then don't support me in the meeting.
   Part IV:　In the future, I want to be able to count on your support because together we can get the proposal approved if we show cooperation.

3. Part I:　I
   Part II:　think the decisions made by the committee should be followed. I feel anxious
   Part III:　when I don't apply the rules they have set.
   Part IV:　In the future, I want to go strictly by the committee's decisions because those were our instructions.

4. Part I:　I
   Part II:　understand that there are times when you must be absent
   Part III:　and lately you have been absent once a week for the past three weeks.
   Part IV:　In the future, I need you here because the work of other people is delayed when you aren't here to do your part.

5. I get irritated when you come into a meeting late, and you have been late for the last two meetings. In the future, I expect you to be on time because you are causing a delay in presenting your information.

6. I get frustrated when you do not return my call. I called on Monday, left a message for you to call me back, and you did not. Please return my calls because I cannot complete my report until I have more information from you.

7. I am angry because you did not compile the information for the Bates report as you were asked to do. As a result, I had to do it for you.

8. I get frustrated when you don't meet a deadline we have set because I cannot complete my work. When you miss a deadline, you cause me to miss mine, and we have missed the last four deadlines. I expect you to meet deadlines in the future.

Chapter Checkpoints

✓ I-statements change an aggressive blaming statement into a non-threatening invitation to discussion.

✓ Creating your own effective I-statements is a positive step toward improving relationships and building self-esteem.

✓ I-statements encourage cooperation and teamwork.

7 | Clarification and Body Language

This chapter will help you to:

- Assert yourself by asking for clarification.
- Recognize the importance of body language in the communication process.

Poor communication skills pose a major obstacle to assertiveness, but as you improve your communication skills, your encounters with others, whether pleasant or unpleasant, should become easier.

Becoming a better communicator starts with I-statements, but requires even more concerted effort and practice. You must also know how to phrase your responses assertively and deliver them with appropriate body language.

ASKING FOR CLARIFICATION

Have you met people who know exactly what to say at the right moment? They know how to "think on their feet" and how to come out of a verbal battle unscathed. These people have learned assertive responses to challenges or disturbing remarks.

Choose Your Words Wisely

You need to choose words carefully when you desire to communicate your thoughts and feelings positively.

Many times, remarks are made to people that cause confusion regarding the speaker's intent. Asking for clarification is one way to decide what a speaker means. The following do's and don'ts will help you become more direct, honest, and respectful. The responses will show you how to phrase questions that force the other person to clarify his or her meaning with specifics.

> I know you believe that you understand what you think I said, but I am not sure you realize that what you heard is not what I meant.
>
> —Author Unknown

Don't Generalize; Use Specifics Instead

The dialogue in the following examples shows the first person violating the rules of clarity and the second person responding assertively by asking for clarification:

When George uses the generalization, "You do poor work," Bill's assertive response is, "In what way is my work poor? Can you give me an example?" George's statement is general. It doesn't describe what he thinks poor work is, nor does it cite a specific example of poor work. Such a general statement is usually seen as aggressive and causes the listener to become defensive.

Bill's response is assertive. He asked for clarification—"In what way is my work poor? Can you give me an example?"

George could have made this assertive statement: "On pages five, six, and seven, you omitted paragraphs, and on page nine you did not check the date."

Don't Be Judgmental

Terry's judgmental statement is: "You are two-faced."

Will's assertive response is: "When have I been two-faced? Can you give me an example along with what was said?"

Terry is being judgmental about Will's character by openly accusing him.

Assuming that Will has not been two-faced, he responds assertively by asking for clarification. He asks for specifics. He doesn't let Terry get away with making such a damaging remark about his character. He asks for an incident that occurred when he was two-faced as well as what was said.

An assertive statement by Terry might have been, "Will, I got angry when Tom told me you had been talking about me behind my back and saying . . . ."

Don't Exaggerate

Joan's statement exaggerates: "When you are constantly away from your desk visiting, yet taking credit for all the work that's done, and expecting me to cover for you, it is more than I can take!"

Ruth's response is assertive: "I didn't know you felt that way. Why didn't you say something to me earlier? When, specifically, have I taken credit for all the work that's been done? And, when, specifically, did you cover for me?"

Joan felt she was doing all the work while Ruth was visiting. Resentment has built up. She may have allowed several instances to occur and has not been assertive by explaining her feelings to Ruth.

Ruth is assertive. She has listened to Joan's exaggerated statement, then expressed that she didn't know how Joan felt. She needed clarification about taking credit and covering for her.

An assertive statement Joan might have said is: "Ruth, when you were away from your desk three times this morning and twice yesterday afternoon, I got frustrated and behind in my work because I had to answer your phone. We are both responsible for the work done in the office. Let's discuss how we can resolve this situation."

Do Accept Responsibility for Your Own Feelings, Thoughts, and Opinions

Dale does not accept responsibility for his emotions. He shouts, "You make me so **!*! mad!"

Dean's response is assertive: "I understand you are angry, but I don't understand what I did to make you angry. What, specifically, did I do?"

Is Dean responsible for Dale's anger? No, Dale is responsible for his own anger. Dale allowed himself to become angry.

When a person is angry and you express understanding and request more information from the person, allowing that person to talk often diffuses his or her anger so that more dialogue can take place.

Dean assertively explained that he understood Dale was angry, but he did not understand what he did to make Dale angry. He asked for clarification. Asking a question, rather than allowing himself to behave emotionally, give in to Dale's anger, and become angry was a correct assertive response to this situation.

Your Turn

Using the following abbreviations, identify each statement accordingly:

G—Generalizing statements.

J—Judgmental statements.

E—Exaggerated statements.

R—Responsibility for feelings, thoughts, and opinions.

Place the appropriate letter in the blanks provided. You may indicate more than one letter for a statement.

_____ 1. "You are such a jerk!"

_____ 2. "My manager is very difficult to work for."

_____ 3. "He makes me so mad!"

_____ 4. "My boss really doesn't appreciate the work I do."

_____ 5. "You never keep your word."

_____ 6. "You tell everything you hear."

_____ 7. "She thinks she is better than everyone else."

_____ 8. "He thinks he knows everything."

_____ 9. "She has an answer for everything."

_____ 10. "He irritates the *!*!* out of me."

Based on the previous 10 statements, rewrite each one as an assertive statement.

1. _____

_____

_____

2. _____

_____

_____

3. _____

_____

_____

4. _____

_____

_____

5. _____

6. _____

7. _____

8. _____

9. _____

10. _____

Next, write an assertive response asking for clarification.

1. _____

2. _____

3. _____

4. _____

5. _____

6. _____

7. _____
_____
_____

8. _____
_____
_____

9. _____
_____
_____

10. _____
_____
_____

BODY LANGUAGE AND COMMUNICATION

By now, you have learned how to express yourself assertively. But there's more. You must display nonverbal behavior—or body language—that supports your assertive statements. Body language includes conscious and unconscious movements in posture, facial expression, gestures, and tone of voice. Staying aware of your body language is very important because the other person is constantly evaluating your messages, by "reading" your body language as well as listening to your words.

Generally 10 percent of your message is received through verbal language. Ninety percent of your message is received through body language. With such a high percentage of your message conveyed by body language, you need to be keenly aware of its effect on the communication process. Note the body language of nonassertive, assertive, and aggressive behaviors shown in the following table.

Compare the following:

Nonassertive	Assertive	Aggressive
Tone of Voice		
Meek, low, timid, anxious, distressed, apologetic, unsure.	Confident, assured, even, steady, modulated, relaxed, calm.	Sarcastic, arrogant, haughty, condescending.

Body Posture

Sagging, stooped shoulders, droopy, wants to appear insignificant.	Well poised, self-assured, leans forward, erect.	High-strung, rigid, taut, firm, edgy.

Facial Expressions

Downcast head and eyes, unsure, bashful, timid.	Direct, genuine, happy, smiling, serious, caring.	Frowning, cold, angry, threatening, staring.

Hand and Arm Gestures

Nervous hands, wringing motions, drooped shoulders, fidgety, fluttery, lots of nervous movement.	Relaxed hand movement, informal, easygoing, spontaneous, unpretentious.	Shaking fist, pointing fingers, quick, angry movements.

Your Turn

Think of situations when you were assertive, aggressive, or nonassertive. Identify the body language you used in each situation.

ASSERTIVE

Situation: _____

_____

Voice: _____

Posture: _____

Facial expressions: _____

Gestures: _____

AGGRESSIVE

Situation: _____

_____

Voice: _____

Posture: _____

Facial expressions: _____

Gestures: _____

NONASSERTIVE

Situation: _____

_____

Voice: _____

Posture: _____

Facial expressions: _____

Gestures: _____

As you've seen, you should choose your words carefully but, at the same time, be aware of how your body language affects what you are saying. Tone of voice, gestures, and so on can greatly affect how the other person understands your meaning—no matter how carefully you select the words. Recall the situation presented in the beginning of the chapter and imagine how body language might affect the meaning in the encounter between Joan and Ruth.

Joan:

> "When you are constantly away from your desk visiting, yet taking credit for all the work that's done, and expecting me to cover for you, it is too much for me to take!"

Ruth:

> "I didn't know you felt that way. Why didn't you say something to me earlier? When, specifically, have I taken credit for all the work that's been done? When did you cover for me?"

Ruth's verbal and body language must express her sincerity and concern, or Joan could easily view her comments as condescending and aggressive. If Ruth had raised her eyebrows, tilted her chin down, lifted her head up and back, and given emphasis to such words as *know, something, I, done,* and *me,* she would have changed her meaning altogether. The change creates a conflict between the body language and the statement being made, and sends a mixed and confusing message.

Y o u r   T u r n

Select a partner and role-play Ruth and Joan's situation. Using the appropriate body language, play Ruth's part aggressively, then assertively.

Assertion vs. Aggression

Next, notice the assertive statement below and see how easily it could have appeared aggressive.

Maria:

> "I get angry when you ask Bryan to work on the Harper report. I'd like you to come to me next time you want the report worked on because it is my responsibility."

When you make this type of assertive statement, you *must* watch your tone of voice. Keep it level—controlled, firm, and relaxed. Do not show emotion, even though you might be angry. In addition, you *must* watch your body language. Keep your head erect and relaxed, have eye contact, and do not point a finger. If you feel you cannot control your anger, defer discussion of the situation until your emotions are under control. When you are in control, you will be able to say the I-statement in such a way that it is not viewed as an attack. In short, you will be communicating more assertively.

Your Turn

Select a partner and role-play Maria's statement. Using the appropriate body language, play Maria's part aggressively, then assertively.

7

Chapter Checkpoints

✓ Become a better communicator by asking for clarification when questionable remarks are made to you.

✓ While the verbal message is important, body language has a greater effect on the message because the sender cannot disguise it.

✓ Body language occurs subconsciously. Only 10 percent of a message is received through words, while 90 percent is received nonverbally.

CHAPTER

8 | Respond Assertively

This chapter will help you to:

- Learn how to accept compliments assertively.
- Learn how to respond to direct and indirect put-downs.

Rewarding people with compliments is a common way to develop positive relationships. Many people, however, have difficulty responding to compliments—they may feel uncomfortable being singled out for praise, or just don't like to be in the spotlight. For some, compliments are unwelcome attention.

Most people would agree that put-downs are definitely unwanted attention. Who likes to be insulted or made the butt of a joke?

As you're building your assertiveness skills, you can learn to respond to both these kinds of attention. It will take practice to face these situations comfortably, but as Ralph Waldo Emerson said, "Courage and confidence come from having repeated a process."

HANDLING COMPLIMENTS ASSERTIVELY

A typical nonassertive or aggressive response to praise might be to shrug off the compliment and think negative self-talk, such as, "I'm not really deserving of a compliment. Anyone would have done the same," or to simply change the subject. The aggressive person might even question the person's motives behind the compliment. Here are some pointers to help you better accept compliments assertively.

- Don't rush to respond to the compliment.
- Think about the compliment (let it soak in).
- Respond to the compliment directly or indirectly through your body language, such as smiling and making good eye contact.
- When all else fails, a simple "thank you" will always do.

A compliment is something like a kiss through a veil.

—Victor Hugo

Consider the following situations for tips on assertive responses to praise:

Situation: A supervisor says, "You really look nice today."

A nonassertive response might be: "This old outfit? I've had it for years."

An aggressive response might be: "Humph!"

Assertive response:
"Well, how nice of you to say that."
"Thank you so much; I needed that lift today."
"Thanks. That is really nice of you to say so."

Situation: A co-worker says, "You are really doing a great job. Congratulations on being employee-of-the-month."

A nonassertive response might be: "Oh, it was really nothing. Everyone provided so much information that I hardly had to do anything at all."

An aggressive response might be (in thoughts or words): "Better me than you."

Assertive responses include:
"Thank you very much. Your praise means a lot to me."
"Thank you, Tom. I appreciate your words of encouragement."
"Thanks. It means a lot when someone genuinely cares."
"Thank you for saying so. Your friendship is really important to me."

Your Turn

In the space provided, create an assertive response to counter the non-assertive response shown.

1. A colleague says: "Congratulations on your recent promotion to office manager!"

   Nonassertive response: "I really didn't think I had a chance at getting the job because I had so little experience."

   Assertive response: _____

8

2. During an evaluation, your boss says: "You are a real asset to our office. I could not be more happy with your work, attitude, and support."

Nonassertive response: Shrug shoulders with mouth shut.

Assertive response:

_____

3. You're wearing a great new suit for the first time, and a colleague says: "Wow, you sure have great taste in clothes!"

Nonassertive response: "Ah, it's nothing, my wife bought it anyway."

Assertive response:

_____

4. You volunteered to be the United Way collector at your office and are working many long hours. The CEO of your company sees you and says, "Thanks for the great job you're doing so far—I realize how committed you are to this worthy cause."

Nonassertive response: "Oh, it is nothing. I feel I should help out when I can."

Assertive response:

_____

HANDLING PUT-DOWNS ASSERTIVELY

Have you ever felt belittled by someone who made a comment about your looks, dress, life-style, mannerisms, work performance, or speech? These put-downs may have made you feel down, embarrassed, worthless, inadequate, incompetent, or incapable even though none of these characteristics describe you.

Types of Put-Downs

Four types of put-downs are:

- Direct verbal put-down.
- Indirect verbal put-down.

- Nonverbal put-down.
- Self put-down.

The Direct Verbal Put-Down.   Of the four types of put-downs, the direct verbal put-down is perhaps the easiest to identify because it is made directly to you.

Situation: Danny and Hollis have been assigned to complete a project for a staff meeting. Danny is more experienced than Hollis and takes the lead in gathering information. Danny and Hollis have worked together on previous projects, but Danny feels that Hollis hasn't done his share of the work in the past. He begins on one part of the project and hands the remaining information to Hollis to continue with the project.

Danny:

[Voice sounding accusing] "You think you can do your part this time?"

Hollis:

"Yes, I will do my part, but I don't understand your statement. Do you have a problem with the way I've done my share of the work in the past?"

Danny has more experience than Hollis and has chosen to take the lead in other projects, but he uses a put-down to let Hollis know that he resents doing more than Hollis.

Here are some pointers for responding to a direct verbal put-down:

- Let the person verbalize his or her feelings.
- Admit when you are wrong.
- State that you understand how the person feels. Use words like "I understand" or "I see that you are upset."
- Ask for clarification if necessary.
- Assert yourself about how the other person is reacting by explaining how you feel about the behavior.
- Make a short statement to bring the situation to an end.

The Indirect Verbal Put-Down.   Have you ever felt that a statement had a double meaning? Here is an example:

8

Dottie:

"Jan, you *actually* made fewer errors this time!"

Jan:

"I don't understand, Jan. What are you really saying?"

Dottie didn't come right out and say, "Jan, you make too many errors." Instead, she indirectly attacked Jan, showing indirect aggression. She tried to achieve her goal by being subtle. Most people have difficulty directly expressing negative feelings about another person's behavior. That is why they camouflage comments by using an indirect put-down.

Jan was confused and may even have been frustrated or felt manipulated. She had to ask for clarification of Dottie's meaning. She put Dottie on the spot to explain her real meaning.

Here are some pointers for handling indirect put-downs. The key is to determine the other person's true intent:

- Ask for clarification.

- Use a statement such as, "I don't understand what you mean."

- Ask questions such as, "What are you saying?"

The Nonverbal Put-Down.   Nonverbal put-downs are more difficult to address because you may doubt your reading of a nonverbal message. Instead of words to deal with, there might be a pout, a "sick" smile, an exasperated sigh, or a smirk. Here is an example:

Situation: The time is 4:30 P.M. and John is supposed to leave at 5 P.M. Amy consistently gives assignments to John just before he is supposed to leave work.

Amy:

"John, here are the letters we discussed before. I need you to type them."

John:

John frowns and gives an exasperated sigh.

Amy is making a simple statement, and she and John discussed the letters previously. Notice that Amy doesn't specifically ask John to type them today. She doesn't understand John's nonverbal language so she asks for clarification.

Amy:

"John, I don't understand your expression."

John assumed Amy needed the letters today and knew he didn't have time to complete the letters without staying late. This situation offers John the opportunity to respond verbally and assertively rather than nonverbally. He should say:

John:

"Amy, do you need these letters today?"

Amy:

"No, tomorrow will be fine."

John:

"Amy, I really get frustrated when you give me work this late in the day. We need to discuss our work schedules so that I can better help you get the work that you need done on time."

Amy:

"That's a good idea, John. When you sighed, I really didn't know what to think. Let's talk about it in the morning."

Here are some pointers for dealing with nonverbal put-downs:

- Ask for clarification if a nonverbal expression isn't clear to you.
- Use the I-statement formula. (Start with I, express your feelings, identify the behavior, and identify what you want from then on.)

The Self Put-Down. Self put-downs involve negative self-talk. Inner conflict and self-doubt can result in your putting yourself down. In this case, you become your own worst enemy by internalizing put-downs.

Situation: Sarah receives a raise for excellent work. Her supervisor compliments her.

Supervisor:

"Sarah, I'm so proud to have you as my assistant. Your work is always top-notch, so I'm recommending a raise for you beginning the first of the month."

Sarah:

"Thank you very much."
(Sarah thinks, "I hope I continue to deserve it.")

8

As you learned earlier, negative self-talk can be damaging to your self-esteem. Say it enough to yourself and you'll believe it. You must be careful to practice positive self-talk. Be honest, open, and straightforward with yourself and, above all, be assertive in your thoughts, feelings, and needs.

Rather than put herself down, Sarah should create positive self-talk and thus build up her self-confidence and self-esteem. Sarah might tell herself "I do deserve that raise—I make valuable contributions every day." In this way, she could avoid the trap of becoming her own adversary.

Your Turn

Describe a situation in which you experienced each type of put-down. Based upon what you have learned, how would you respond now?

1. Direct verbal put-down:

_____
_____
_____
_____

2. Indirect verbal put-down:

_____
_____
_____
_____

3. Nonverbal put-down:

_____
_____
_____
_____

4. Self put-down:

_____
_____
_____
_____

Write your assertive response to the following put-downs in the space provided.

1. "How about trying to carry your weight around here for a change?"

_____

_____

_____

2. "Well, is the report *finally* finished, Mr. Speedo?"

_____

_____

_____

3. "I didn't know *you ever* tried to learn new things."

_____

_____

_____

4. Under your breath you hear her say: "Good grief, not again!"

_____

_____

_____

8

8

Chapter Checkpoints

When you respond to compliments:

✓ Don't rush to return the compliment.

✓ Think about the compliment; then respond directly or indirectly through your body language.

✓ Smile and make good eye contact.

✓ Put-downs leave you feeling embarrassed, inadequate, and down. Build your self-esteem by dealing with them assertively.

Post-Test

Now that you've worked through the book, respond to the following statements to assess your current assertiveness skills. Congratulations on developing and sharpening these skills!

	Almost Always	Sometimes	Almost Never
1. I can easily compliment a peer, friend, or family member.	_____	_____	_____
2. I can openly express my feelings to others.	_____	_____	_____
3. I can admit to making a mistake.	_____	_____	_____
4. I can easily ask for clarification.	_____	_____	_____
5. I can say no when someone makes a completely unfair demand of me.	_____	_____	_____
6. I can tell people I don't like their behavior.	_____	_____	_____
7. I can assertively answer a verbal put-down.	_____	_____	_____
8. I can assert myself when someone takes credit for my ideas.	_____	_____	_____
9. I can tell another person when he or she has done something that has offended me.	_____	_____	_____
10. I know what to say when I receive a compliment.	_____	_____	_____
11. I can choose my own life-style even though others may disagree.	_____	_____	_____
12. I can maintain eye contact when expressing my feelings, wants, and needs.	_____	_____	_____
13. When I get mad, I can express myself without showing anger, frustration, or disappointment.	_____	_____	_____
14. I can deal with conflict constructively.	_____	_____	_____
15. I can ask others for help.	_____	_____	_____
16. I can easily express my disagreements and opinions.	_____	_____	_____
17. I can ask for clarification of a nonverbal expression.	_____	_____	_____
18. I use I-statements rather than *you* statements.	_____	_____	_____
19. I can accept compliments.	_____	_____	_____
20. I feel confident in my skills and abilities.	_____	_____	_____

THE BUSINESS SKILLS EXPRESS SERIES

This growing series of books addresses a broad range of key business skills and topics to meet the needs of employees, human resource departments, and training consultants.

To obtain information about these and other Business Skills Express books, please call Business One IRWIN toll free at: 1-800-634-3966.

Effective Performance Management	ISBN	1-55623-867-3
Hiring the Best	ISBN	1-55623-865-7
Writing that Works	ISBN	1-55623-856-8
Customer Service Excellence	ISBN	1-55623-969-6
Writing for Business Results	ISBN	1-55623-854-1
Powerful Presentation Skills	ISBN	1-55623-870-3
Meetings that Work	ISBN	1-55623-866-5
Effective Teamwork	ISBN	1-55623-880-0
Time Management	ISBN	1-55623-888-6
Assertiveness Skills	ISBN	1-55623-857-6
Motivation at Work	ISBN	1-55623-868-1
Overcoming Anxiety at Work	ISBN	1-55623-869-X
Positive Politics at Work	ISBN	1-55623-879-7
Telephone Skills at Work	ISBN	1-55623-858-4
Managing Conflict at Work	ISBN	1-55623-890-8
The New Supervisor: Skills for Success	ISBN	1-55623-762-6
The *Americans with Disabilities Act*: What Supervisors Need to Know	ISBN	1-55623-889-4